TWELVE MOONS

A Year with the Sauk and Meskwa

...de possible through the
...following:
...etta Young Trust
The Charles Deere Wiman Trust
The Citizens to Preserve Black Hawk Park Foundation
The Community Foundation of the Great River Bend
The Moline Foundation
The Riverboat Development Authority
Gifts from friends of Black Hawk State Historic Site

We would like to extend our thanks to members of the Meskwaki Nation and Sauk Nation for their assistance in authenticating the many details of tribal life. Thanks to Janet and Norm Moline for their invaluable editing. Thanks to Steve Leonard of the Illinois Historic Preservation Agency whose work with the Hauberg Museum helped to initiate the idea for this project. The author would also like to extend his appreciation to his daughter Katie Willcockson whose exceptional coloring skills contributed enormously to the project's final completion, and to his wife Terry for her loving support and advice.

We invite readers of all ages to visit and enjoy the wide array of educational activities at the Black Hawk State Historic Site and the Hauberg Museum in Rock Island.

Sources:

Original sources consulted for this book include: Thomas Forsyth's narratives; ethnographies of the Sauk and Meskwaki Indians; *The Territorial Papers of the United States*; *The Atlas of the Great Lakes Indians*; *The Handbook of Native Americans*; *The Autobiography of Black Hawk*; paintings and lithographs by Karl Bodmer, George Catlin, and Henry Schoolcraft; exhibits at the Hauberg Museum; and exhibits at the Museum of Natural History at the University of Iowa.

Websites:

www.blackhawkpark.org
www.sacandfoxnation-nsn.gov
www.meskwaki.org
www.mapcraft.com

Copyright:

Pre-press and printing by Woolverton, Cedar Falls, Iowa

ISBN 978-0-615-62273-6

TWELVE MOONS

A Year with the Sauk and Meskwaki, 1817-1818

Tom Willcockson

Text by Elizabeth Carvey

INTRODUCTION

Did you ever wonder what life was like for the native people who lived here before us? This book tells the story of the Sauk and Meskwaki people, following them through one year, 1817 to 1818.

The Sauk and Meskwaki were the last two tribes of native people who occupied the 400 miles of the Mississippi River valley from the Wisconsin River to the Missouri River. They lived here from 1735 to 1831. They had not always lived here. The two tribes originated in eastern Canada. Many centuries ago they were forced from their native lands by the Iroquois. The Sauk and Meskwaki slowly migrated westward, and by the 1650's were living along Green Bay and the Fox River in what is now Wisconsin. They first met French fur traders and missionaries in 1666, forever changing their way of life. In 1700 the French and Meskwaki became involved in trade wars which lasted for more than thirty years. By 1733 the French had killed most of the Meskwaki. In order to survive, the Sauk and Meskwaki became allies. Together they left their Wisconsin homes and moved to the upper Mississippi River valley. Here they found a place rich in natural resources; land good for growing crops, forests, rivers and prairies, all filled with plants and animals that guaranteed an abundant living. This land was offered to them by Creator and was a place where they would remain.

The Sauk and Meskwaki ordered their lives by the cycle of the seasons, performing different tasks at different times of the year. In the summer they lived together in large towns growing the crops that provided food for the coming year. After the harvest in the fall, they left their towns, broke up into smaller groups called bands and scattered for the winter to hunt. In the late winter the men continued hunting while the women went to the maple groves to make their year's supply of maple sugar. When the sugaring season was done, the different bands returned to their towns to begin the cycle over again. They had lived this age old rhythm of life for as long as they could remember.

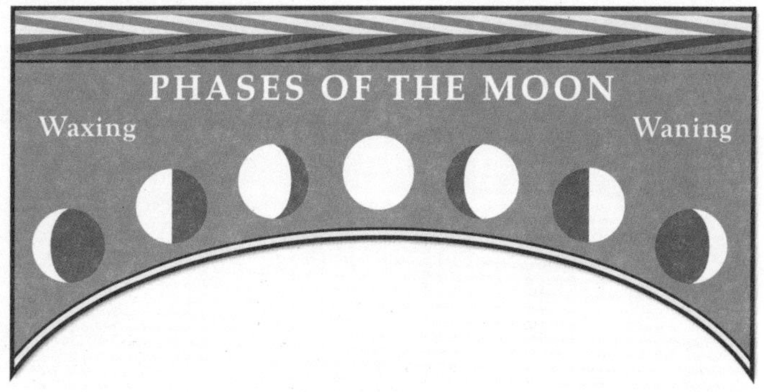

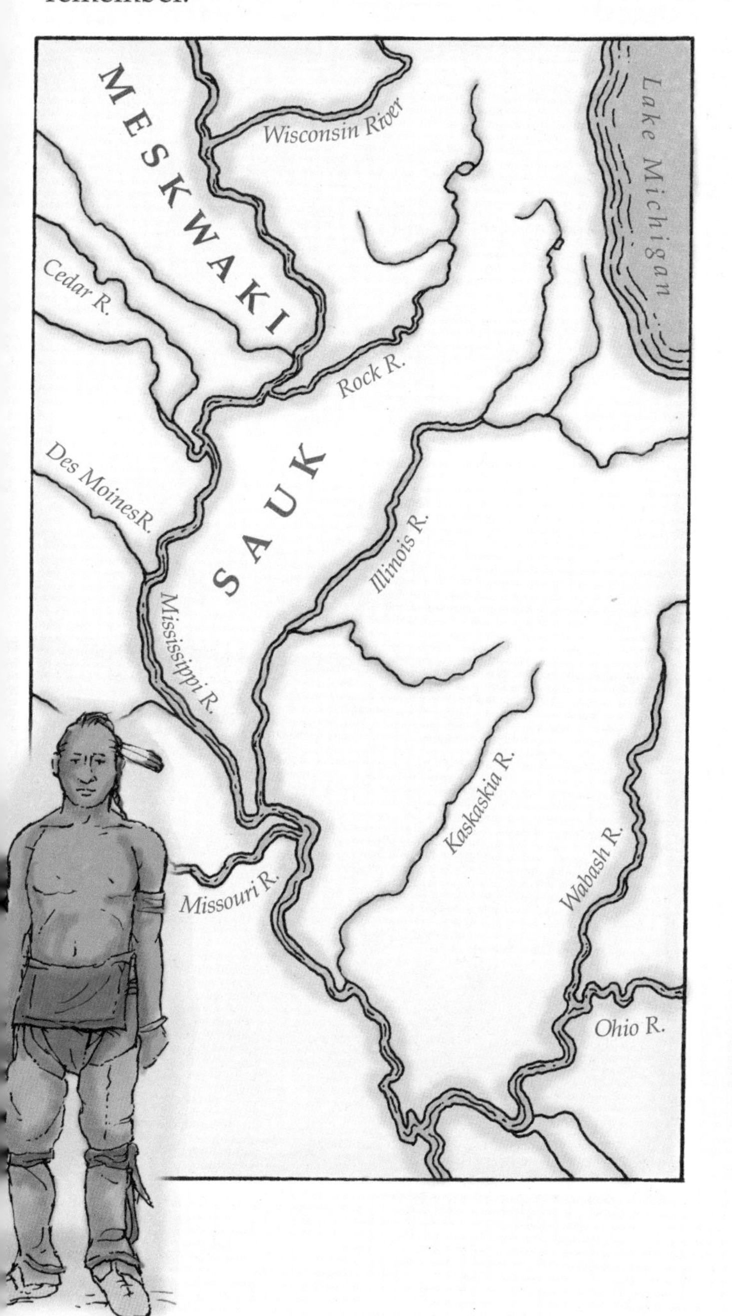

The Sauk and Meskwaki had no clocks or calendars. They measured time by the phases of the moon. Each lunar month began with the new moon and ended when that moon had "died." They also regulated their activities by the movement of the stars and had names for the major stars and constellations. The lunar month and the seasonal positions of the stars told the people when it was time to plant and harvest their crops, when it was time to depart for the winter hunt and the sugaring camps, and when it was time to meet on the Mississippi to return to their summer towns and start their year over again. The lunar months are the format used for timekeeping in this book. The story begins at the end of the sugaring season, in March 1817.

THE GATHERING

Winter was over! The sap had stopped flowing out from the maple trees, the buds on the trees were starting to open, the ice was breaking up in the rivers, and the first frogs could be heard croaking. The Sauk and Meskwaki were waiting for these signs which meant it was time to leave their sugar camps and meet up with other members of their tribe to prepare to return to their summer towns.

It had been many months since everyone had been together. Last autumn the Sauk and Meskwaki tribes had broken up into many bands and dispersed into their hunting lands. Two months ago, during Cold Moon, the hunting bands had divided. The young men left to hunt beaver and bear. The women, children, and elderly went to the maple groves to make their year's supply of maple sugar. Now the sugar makers were coming to the rendezvous point on the Mississippi River where they would await the return of the hunters.

People hurried into the clearing, calling out greetings to friends and family members. Those who had gotten there first had built their shelters. The cattail mats and red elm bark that were used to cover these homes had gotten a bit ragged. They had been in constant use for the past several months and were wearing out. They needed to last just a few more weeks. Soon the people would return to their summer towns and would move back into their more sturdy summer homes.

Groups of hunters began to appear, bringing fresh meat with them. The women and children

were glad to see them. Soon a great feast would celebrate the end of winter, a successful hunt, and a good sugaring season. Once all were gathered, had feasted and given thanks, it would be time to move to the Yellow Banks, where they would cross the Mississippi River to its eastern side and begin the journey home.

Up and down the river other bands of Sauk and Meskwaki were gathering in the same way. All remained at their rendezvous points for the next few weeks until everyone had arrived and the signs told them it was time to move on to their summer towns once again.

YELLOW BANKS

Tobacco

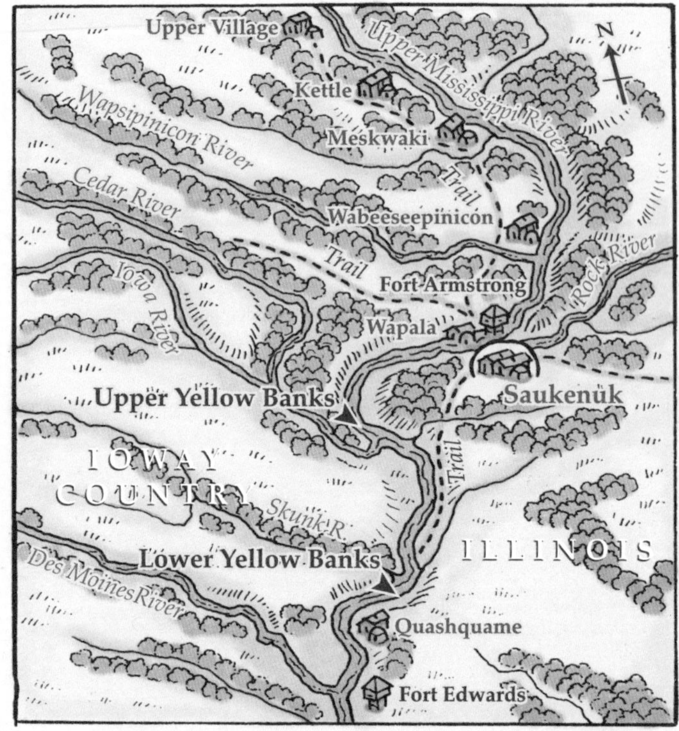

Map of the Upper Mississippi River

The first sliver of Fish Moon could be seen in the night sky. The different hunting bands had met on the western shore of the Mississippi at a place called Lower Yellow Banks. This was a good place to cross the river. Many islands broke up the strong river currents making it easier to move people and equipment across to the other side. The spring floods had receded, and the river could be crossed with care. Before crossing, offerings of tobacco were made to the river's Guardian Spirit. The Mississippi was a powerful river, and strong currents and snags of floating stumps and trees made the crossing challenging and dangerous.

The women, children, and elderly were ferried across in dugout canoes. They carefully made their way through the many islands and wetlands. The young men guided the horses that

Migrating Geese

were swimming across the channels from island to island. As the people made their way across the river, they saw flocks of geese, cranes, pelicans, ducks, and pigeons crowding the skies. They were migrating from their winter homes in the south along the great river flyway to their summer homes in the north. The air was deafening at times with their calls.

Encampments were set up on the east side of the river to shelter those who had crossed successfully. Once everyone had crossed, they waited for other hunting bands to join them. When everyone had arrived, they took the ancient trail leading north through the broad river valley and up the gently sloping hills to where the Rock River met the Mississippi. It was an orderly march. They progressed about ten miles per day, moving only on days when the weather was good. Rainy days were spent in camp. Young men kept the group together, safe from mishap or attack by enemies. Other young men scouted ahead and set up camp sites for the night's rest. The people were looking forward to returning to their summer towns. They had been away for a long time.

SENISEPO KEBESAUKEE

By 1817 the Sauk and Meskwaki had lived in the Mississippi River valley for over eighty years. They were two separate tribes who were linked through language, customs, traditions, and marriage. They lived in separate towns along a 200 mile stretch of the Mississippi River. The capital towns of the two nations were built on the peninsula formed by the confluence of the Rock and Mississippi Rivers.

The people called this land Senisepo Kebesaukee. The Sauk lived along the Rock River about two miles above its mouth in a large city called Saukenuk. The Meskwaki lived in a smaller town, known as Wapala's town, on the Mississippi River about four miles north of the Sauk. A trail connected the two towns. Other trails leading in and out from the towns made the area a transportation center.

The region was suited to their every need for survival. The two tribes grew corn, beans, and squash on the gentle slopes called bluffs that ran north and south between their towns. Underground springs located near their towns provided drinking water. They used the natural resources found in the nearby forests, rivers,

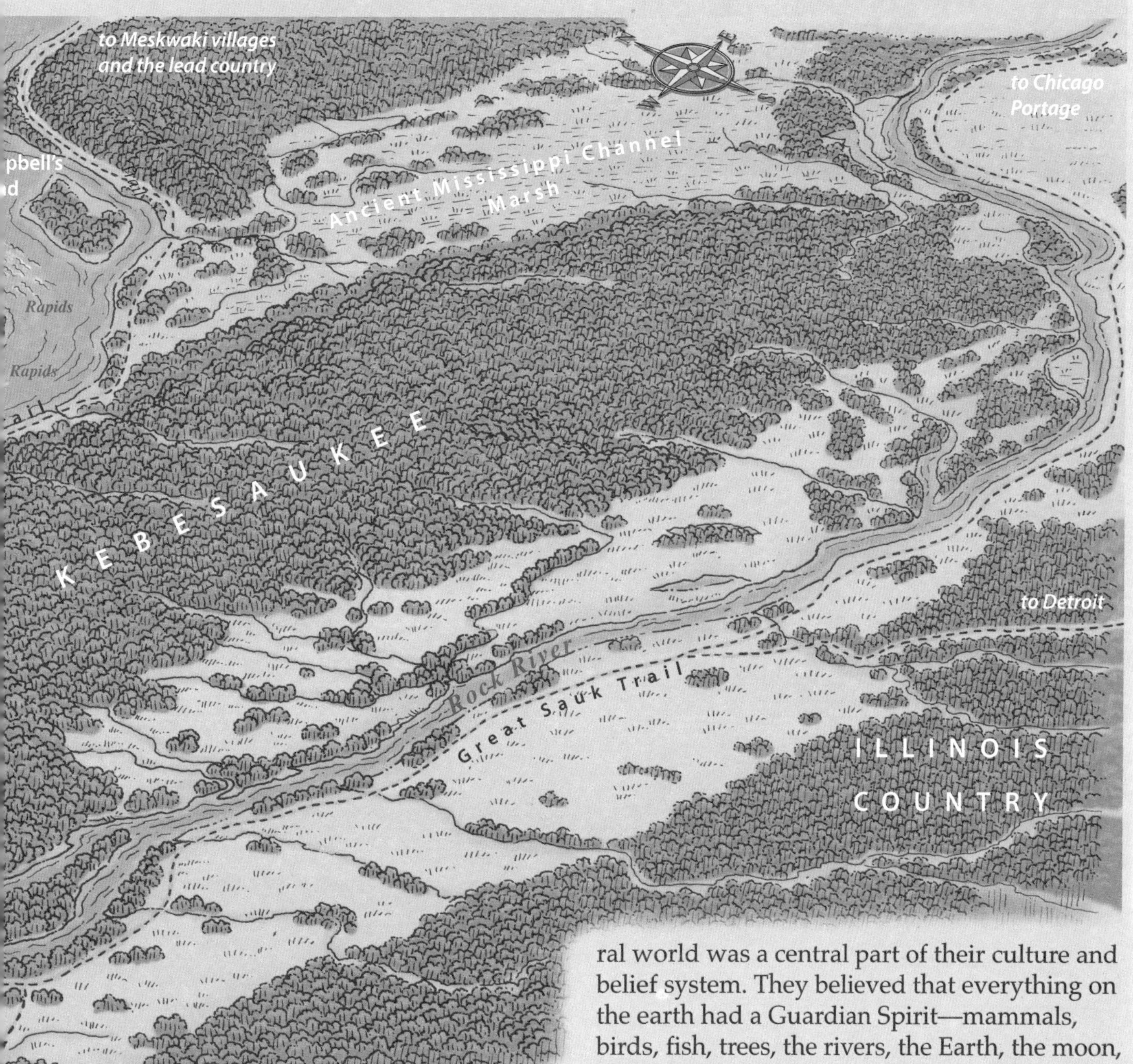

and prairies. The upland forests offered building materials, food, medicine, and clothing. The prairie to the west of the Mississippi River provided food and medicine. The rivers provided easy transportation in all directions. Ducks and fish were hunted for food, and the cattails and reeds that grew in the fresh water marshes provided materials for making mats.

The Sauk and Meskwaki were tied to the land both physically and spiritually. The natural world was a central part of their culture and belief system. They believed that everything on the earth had a Guardian Spirit—mammals, birds, fish, trees, the rivers, the Earth, the moon, the sun, the air, and even the rocks. The people were mindful of these Spirits in everything they did, including planting their crops, hunting animals, and gathering the plants that were used for food and medicine. The cycle of the seasons by which they lived was evident in the natural world around them. It was evident in the cycle of a day, in the cycle of the moon, and in the cycle of the stars in the sky. All the earth and its plants and animals were tied together in a cycle that never ended.

SAUKENUK

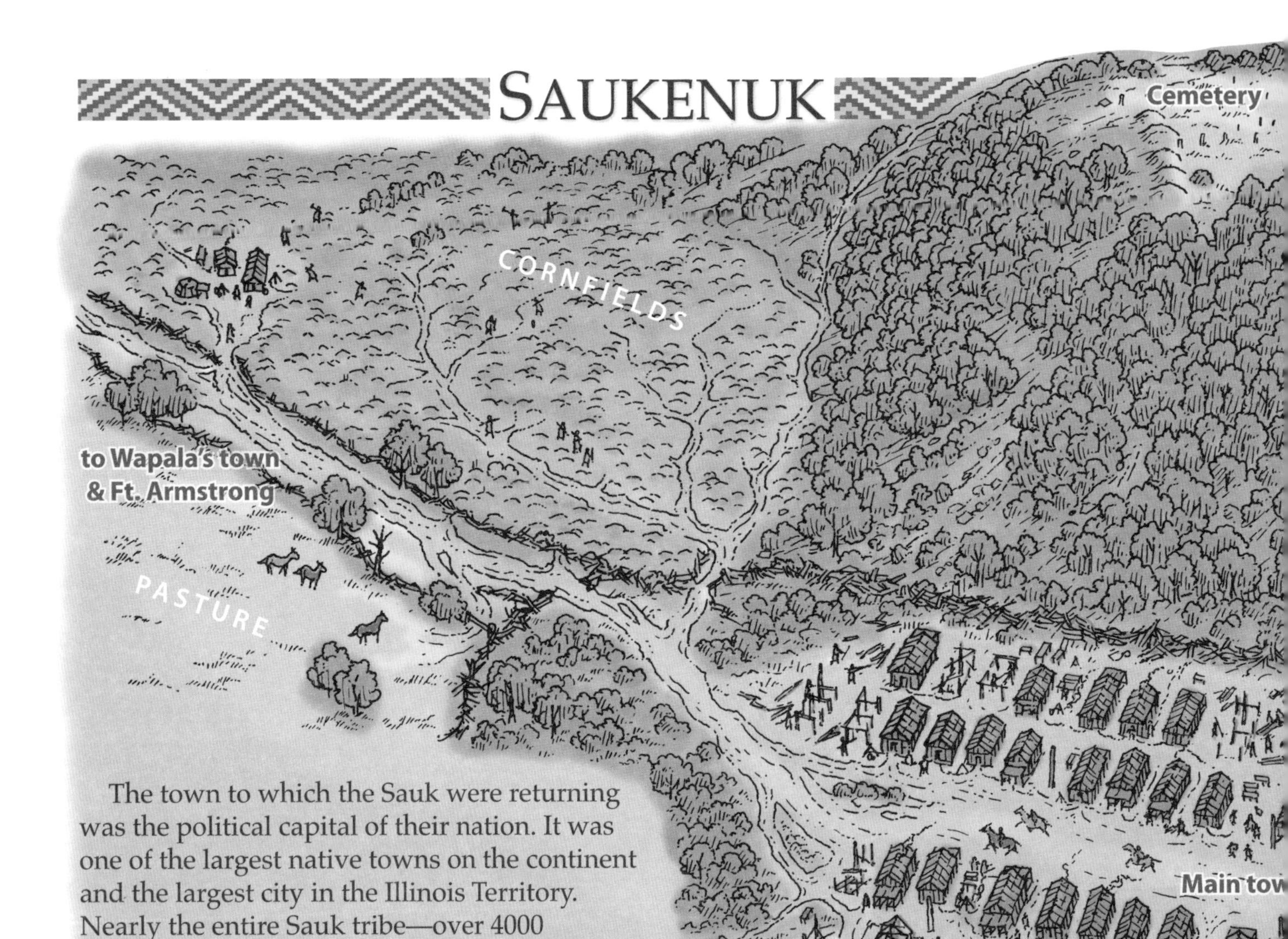

The town to which the Sauk were returning was the political capital of their nation. It was one of the largest native towns on the continent and the largest city in the Illinois Territory. Nearly the entire Sauk tribe—over 4000 people—lived there. This size was unusual. Most native towns contained no more than a few hundred people but the Sauk lived together for defensive purposes.

Saukenuk, like all Sauk and Meskwaki summer towns, was laid out in an organized grid fashion. A main avenue ran north and south through the middle of town and was crossed by side streets going east and west. One hundred long houses faced the streets. The town was divided into neighborhoods, one for each of the twelve clans: Bear, Wolf, Bald Eagle, Sturgeon, Thunder, Ringed Perch, Bear Potato, Great Lake, Deer, Panther, Black Bass, and Swan. Each neighborhood contained a clan house where important functions took place.

The chiefs and clan leaders met in the large Council House that stood at the south end of town. A large open area called a plaza was located in front of the Council House. The whole tribe gathered in the plaza for national meetings, dances, games, and other ceremonies.

The cornfields started at the north end of town. They extended north to where they joined those of the Meskwaki. Across from the cornfields was pasture for the horses.

Large cemeteries were located on the bluffs directly above Saukenuk. Smaller cemeteries were located throughout the town.

As Fish Moon reached the full stage, the Sauk returned to Saukenuk, some crossing at the ford near the Council House, others arriving by canoe. It was good to be home! People hurried to their houses. Over the next several

weeks the people would be busy reclaiming the town that had been empty for the last seven months. Houses needed to be repaired, and some new ones built. The cornfields had to be prepared for planting. Soon all of the hunters would be back, too. A lot of work had to be done, but once it was over, the feasting and dancing could begin.

RECLAIMING THE TOWN

Harvesting elm bark

Seven months was a long time to be away from home. As the people returned, they moved back into their long houses that had been empty all winter. The women cleaned out the leaves and other debris that had blown inside while they were gone. Items that had been taken with them during the winter were stored away. Any mats still usable were spread on the beds and floors. Some of the bark wall and roof coverings had to be replaced.

This year many new houses were being built. Women built the houses. Aided by older children, they went to the nearby forest to collect the materials needed. Cedar trees were best for the large posts that supported the house. Cedar did not rot easily. Long oak or walnut saplings were needed to create the house frame and roof

Repairing and building summer houses

Opening a cache pit

rafters. Elm bark was needed to cover the roof and walls. Basswood bark fiber was needed to make the rope that tied everything together.

Groups of women headed to the forests to get fresh elm bark. Fish Moon was the best time to collect the bark because the sap flow made the job easier. The bark was removed from live trees. The tree was girdled or cut all the way around at the base of the tree and as high as the women could reach. They cut the bark lengthwise and used stone and metal tools to peel it away in large rolls. The bark rolls were heated over a fire and then flattened under stones. The bark pieces now were ready to be tied in place.

Some of the women opened the pits or caches where last fall's dried vegetables and seeds had been stored. The clay-topped, waterproof pits had protected the dried foods and seeds. No mold had grown on them, and no mice or insects had gotten in. Now they had food to eat and seeds to plant.

The men repaired the fences that surrounded the cornfields and horse pastures. Horses were gaining importance among the Sauk and Meskwaki. For over sixty years they had traded for horses with western tribes. Horses allowed the people to travel great distances at rapid speeds.

This season was also the time to bury those who had died during the winter. Graves were prepared in the different cemeteries. Grave posts, painted with clan symbols, were put up at the head of the grave. Four days of mourning followed the funeral during which time the deceased's name was not spoken. Close family members mourned for a longer time, blackening their faces with charcoal and giving away their possessions so that Creator would take pity on them for their suffering. When the mourning period ended, the relatives put on their best clothes and painted their faces. In time another person was adopted into the family to take the place of the deceased.

During this time everyone visited the graves of their ancestors. They hoed away the grass that had grown over the grave and swept it clean. The grave post was freshly painted, and often an offering of food and tobacco was left at the grave. It was an important responsibility and source of comfort to all the people.

Cemetery

SPRING PLANTING

Planting Moon had arrived. The leaves on the oak trees were the size of a little finger. The mayapples were blooming in the forest. It was time to plant the corn. The Sauk and Meskwaki grew over 800 acres of corn, beans, squash, melons, and pumpkins, enough to feed their people for an entire year. They also grew tobacco, a sacred plant that was needed for their prayers, official acts, and other ceremonial purposes.

Only the women farmed. The farm fields were held in common, and no land could be given away or sold without their permission. The Sauk and Meskwaki believed that women had a special relationship with the Earth because the Spirit of the Earth was female. Both the women and the Spirit had the ability to bring new life into the world.

The women grew the corn and beans together in large hills or mounds. The same hill was used every year. The women prepared the fields for planting by scraping away last year's dead plants and digging up the hill. Each seed of corn was planted by hand. Corn was the most important crop they grew and was considered to have its own Guardian Spirit. It provided more

Preparing the corn fields

Corn

Pumpkin

Bean

energy than any other plant and gave the people strength and endurance. Ten days later they planted the beans. As the beans grew, they climbed up the cornstalks. The beans put nutrients into the soil that the corn needed to grow. Squash, melons, and pumpkins were planted between the hills. As they grew, they spread out choking out the weeds and keeping the soil moist. Girls helped their mothers plant and care for the crops. Young boys were armed with bows and arrows, patrolling the land and shooting at any animals or birds that got into the fields. In this way the boys practiced their hunting skills and helped to protect their families' food source. The farmers lived in the cornfields throughout the summer in houses located in the fields. This custom saved the long walk to and from the fields and meant that someone was always there to protect and care for the crops.

Tending the crops

SOCIETY AND CEREMONY

Hunters feasting

During Planting Moon the last of the hunters returned to the summer towns, and now the whole population was gathered together again. While the women were busy putting the long houses in order and planting the cornfields, the men feasted and talked about their experiences on the winter hunt. They discussed news of the region—other tribes they had seen over the winter and the political situation with the Americans. They waited for the planting to be finished. Once that was done, the clan feasts and dancing could begin.

Both the Sauk and Meskwaki tribes were divided into large family groups called clans. They were based on traditional family relationships of birth, marriage, and adoption. Children were born into their father's clan and were named from a list of names identified with the clan's Guardian Spirit. Marriage within the clan was forbidden.

Each tribe was divided into two groups called moieties. Children were assigned alternately to a moiety at birth so that brothers and sisters could be in different moieties. Moieties crossed clan lines too, providing unity within the nation. Members of one moiety painted

themselves with black paint, the other moiety used white. The moieties provided ready made teams for sports and mock battles. Each had a leader whose job it was to mobilize the moiety in times of national emergency.

When the fields were planted, many days of feasting and dancing could begin. It was a time to celebrate and to reconnect with family and friends after the long winter separation.

The Crane Dance was held first. A feast was given and then they danced. The men began the dance, and soon many young women joined in, dressed in their best clothing and decorated with feathers. During this dance a young man might make it known to a woman that he loved her and wanted to marry. When a man had chosen a bride, he told his mother. She approached the mother of the bride, and the two families discussed the marriage possibilities. If they decided it was a good match, the groom's family provided the bride's family with gifts. Next, the man played love songs on a special courting flute whenever his intended was nearby. One night, as she slept, he came to her house holding a light. He woke her up and held the light to his face so that she would know him. If she blew it out, she accepted him and they were considered married.

After the Crane Dance was over, it was time to feast again and dance the Warrior's Dance. The chiefs and old warriors seated themselves on mats in front of the plaza. The drummers and singers took their places. Men and women lined the sides of the plaza. One by one the warriors came into the center of the plaza and through dance recounted the battles they had fought. It was a way of teaching a warrior's knowledge, tactics, and skills to the young men and boys and a way to relive past successes.

THE LONG HOUSE

The long house was at the center of Sauk and Meskwaki family life. It was built, maintained, and owned by the women. The women set and enforced strict rules and customs for behavior within the house. Extended families lived in each house, from grandparents to all the grand-children. As many as fifty people lived in the larger houses. Extended family relationships were a critical part of Sauk and Meskwaki culture. Aunts, uncles, and grandparents had important roles in educating the children, teaching them adult life skills, religion, history, and traditional ways of living. Grandmothers cared for babies and toddlers. The families divided the work which made life easier. Some farmed, some collected medicinal plants, and some wove mats. The men hunted to provide meat and shared it equally among everyone. Children helped their mothers and other female relatives to perform their daily chores. Children were treated with great respect. It was a common belief that spirits chose the family into which they were born; thus, a birth meant a great honor had been bestowed upon the parents and family.

Benches, measuring three feet high and four feet wide, lined the long sides of the house. The benches were covered with reed mats and animal skins for comfort. They provided a place to sit during the day and a place to sleep at night. Personal belongings were stored underneath the benches and in the rafters above. The floors were covered with a smooth, hard layer of clay. Reed mats covered the floors. Doorways were located at the east and west sides of the house facing the direction of both the rising and setting

sun. Fire pits were located in the wide center aisle of the house. Each house contained between two and five fires, depending on the number of families living there. Each individual family occupied the space around its fire pit. Reed mats were hung between the individual family living spaces to provide some privacy. Open air platforms were built outside the doorway. Cooking fires were located beneath them so that the heat of the fire did not make it uncomfortable inside on hot summer days.

The women did all of the cooking. Their families especially liked bear and venison meat. A favorite dish consisted of roasted venison dipped in a mixture of melted bear fat and maple sugar. Sometimes they made a vegetable dish of corn, beans, and pumpkins cooked together and flavored with maple sugar. In the late summer they boiled sweet corn together with duck or turkey. But most food was made into soup. A pot of soup always was hanging over the fire, and people ate whenever they were hungry. Everyone used their own wooden bowl and spoon for everyday meals. When invited to a feast, people brought special bowls and spoons with them.

THE COUNCIL HOUSE

A Council House was located in every Sauk and Meskwaki summer town. It served as the seat of government where the chiefs and Tribal Council met to discuss affairs of state. Visiting dignitaries from other nations were received there. The Council House was twice the size of the largest long house. Benches, covered with reed mats and soft furs, were built along three sides of the structure.

The Sauk and Meskwaki were governed by hereditary chiefs. Sauk civil chiefs were chosen from the Sturgeon Clan. Meskwaki civil chiefs were chosen from the Bear Clan. Some of the chiefs had national standing while others were minor chiefs at the head of a particular town or band.

The Tribal Council was composed of the various clan leaders with the civil chiefs presiding. The role of the Council was to conduct treaty negotiations, accept or reject alliances with other Indian nations, and assign winter hunting lands. Council meetings were called when a question or crisis concerning the nation arose. The Council members discussed the issue, sometimes for days on end, at which point a decision for action was made. The decision had to be unanimous, but even then it was only a recommendation. Council decisions were not binding on the nation. It was the job of the chiefs and Council members to persuade the nation to accept their decision.

Wampum belts, woven from colored beads made into a pattern, and pipes were used as a means of diplomacy between different nations. They symbolized official acts; serving as an invitation for an alliance, an intent to go to war, or peaceful intentions. Emissaries from other

out but could not stop them. In 1817 warfare occurred between different native nations and concerned territorial disputes or acts of revenge. The Sauk and Meskwaki were in strict alliance with each other, if one group were attacked, the other came to its defense. Prisoners of war were treated well. Some were adopted into the nation, and others were kept for exchange or ransom.

Embassy to Fort Malden.

nations were received at the Council House. They delivered speeches to the Council, words their own chiefs had spoken, and presented the wampum belt and pipe with a request for an alliance. If the Sauk and Meskwaki accepted the alliance, they kept the belt and smoked the pipe. If the alliance was rejected, then the pipe and belt were returned.

Warfare was an important part of Sauk and Meskwaki society. Warriors were men of status and important decisions concerning the nation needed their approval. Meskwaki war chiefs were chosen from the Fox Clan. The Sauk had no formal war chiefs; any warrior with a good plan could lead a war party. Sometimes a war party was sent out at the request of the Tribal Council. At other times the war parties acted independently of the Council and even went against their wishes. In such cases the Council worked to dissuade the war party from setting

Organizing a war party

Capturing horses

Axe and war bundle

SUMMER LANDS

First Summer Moon was growing towards the full stage. The corn was planted, and the late spring feasts were over. Now many of the Sauk and Meskwaki left their summer towns, and were gone for the next two months. The farmers and young children remained behind with a few old men left in charge. The chiefs visited American officials in St. Louis and other native tribes from whom they obtained horses. Others went to visit the British in Canada. Most of those who left, though, spread out into their territory to harvest the natural resources there.

The valleys and slopes east of the Mississippi were covered by deep forests. Oaks and hickories dominated, but black walnut, basswood, maple, and cherry trees also were abundant. The animals and plants in the forests provided the Sauk and Meskwaki with food, medicines, and building materials for their homes.

The land west of the Mississippi River was dominated by the tall grass prairie that was located in the uplands between the rivers that crossed the region. The prairie was made up of tall grasses and wild flowers, and teemed with elk, buffalo, and prairie fowl. Prairies were found in this region because native people set fire to the prairie to encourage the growth of the plants that fed the elk and buffalo. The fires destroyed most trees. Trees still could be found along the banks of the rivers and streams.

Many rivers emptied into the Mississippi River. The rivers provided the people's main means of transportation, allowing them to travel easily in every direction. Marshes with grasses and swamps with trees were found along the rivers. The rivers and marshes provided food and materials to make mats.

Lead ore deposits were found in the area between the Wisconsin and Apple Rivers east of the Mississippi and between the Turkey and Little Maquoketa Rivers on the west. Native people had mined these deposits for a very long time, trading the ore to other tribes. Now the Sauk and Meskwaki mined the lead ore and used it to buy goods from their traders.

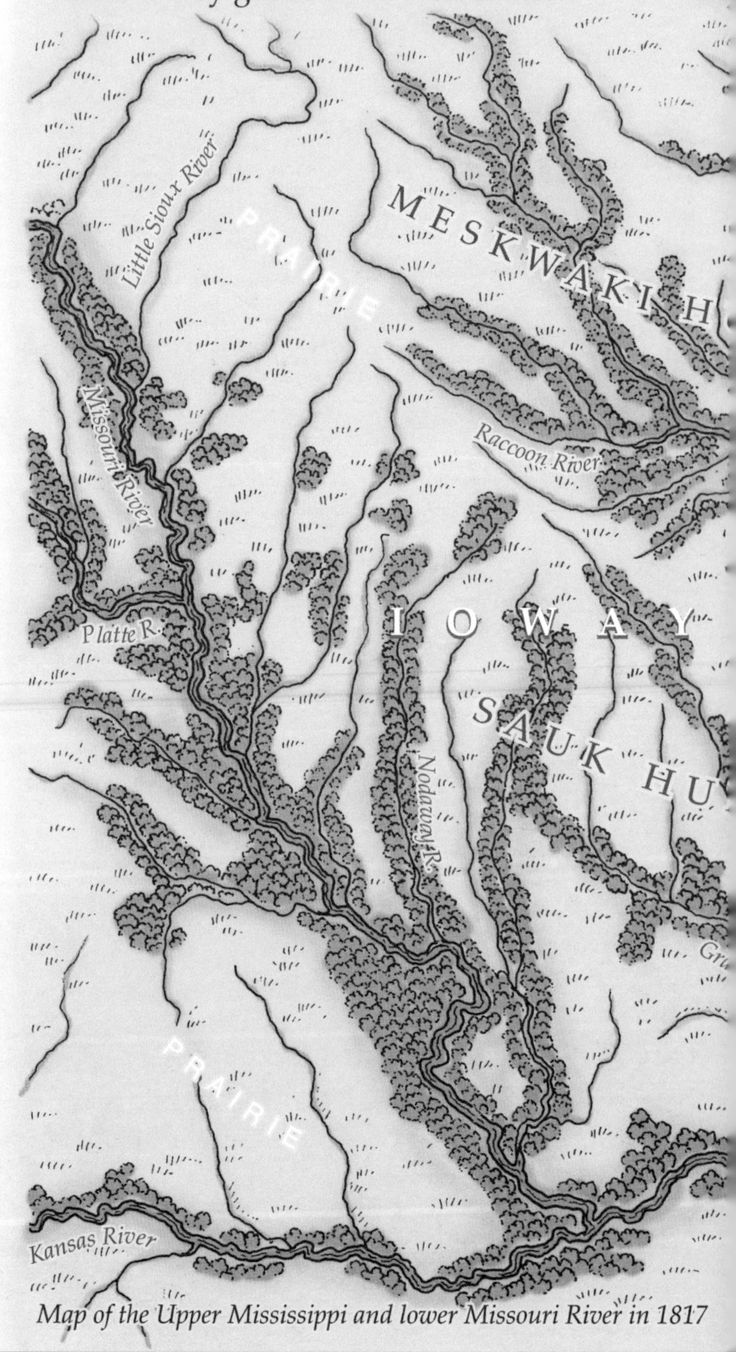

Map of the Upper Mississippi and lower Missouri River in 1817

Upper Mississippi River
FOREST
WINNEBAGO
Fox River
Lake Oshkosh
Lake Michigan
Portage
MESKWAKI
Meskwaki
Fort Crawford
Wisconsin River
Turkey R.
POTAWATOMI
FOREST
Lead deposits
Lead deposits
Upper Village
Kettle
Meskwaki
Wapsipinicon River
Cedar River
Trail
Fort Dearborn
Chicago Portage
Fox River
Iowa River
Wabeeseepinicon
Rock River
Marsh
G GROUNDS
Fort Armstrong
Wapala
to Detroit & Fort Malden
Great Sauk Trail
Upper Yellow Banks
Saukenuk
Skunk River
Des Moines River
Trail
SAUK
Illinois River
COUNTRY
PRAIRIE
Fort Madison (in ruins)
Fort Clark (in ruins)
Quashquame
Lower Yellow Banks
Fort Edwards
FOREST
G GROUNDS
Mississippi River
Salt Creek
Sauk
ILLINOIS
TERRITORY
MISSOURI
TERRITORY
Boones Lick
Edwardsville
St. Charles
SHAWNEE
Missouri River
St. Louis
Cahokia

PRAIRIE

The prairie environment was new to the Sauk and Meskwaki. They had lived on forested land for as long as they could remember, but since moving to the Mississippi River valley in 1735, they had learned to make use of the prairie. The tall grass prairie that covered much of their hunting territories was a vast sea of grass and flowers, with only a few trees dotting the landscape. Buffalo trails were used by the people to travel easily through the tall grass. The Sauk and Meskwaki had learned the medicinal uses of the plants that grew there. They had learned to hunt prairie chickens, bobwhites, and other prairie birds. They had learned to hunt bison, or buffalo as they were commonly called. As First Summer Moon came to an end, large groups of hunters prepared to go on the buffalo hunt. The buffalo now lived only far west of the Mississippi River. Horses allowed the Sauk and Meskwaki to travel to these more distant hunting lands.

Before setting out, the buffalo hunters danced the Buffalo Head Dance. The lead dancer wore a full sized buffalo head and led the hunters in a line through town, dancing in time to the beat of the drum and the voices of the singers. Other townspeople joined the line and the dancers wound their way through the streets of the town and beyond. They were calling to the Spirit of the buffalo, enticing it to come forward so that the hunters would be successful.

Buffalo Head Dance

As the hunters prepared to leave, they packed their horses with the supplies they would need while gone. Deerskin bags full of dried corn, dried beans, and maple sugar were loaded onto the horses. Men brought their guns and butchering knives. Axes were packed to be used for cutting firewood at the camps along the way. They packed containers of bear fat which they used as an insect repellant. They packed their bowls and spoons for eating and

Pack saddle

containers holding hot coals to enable them to start a fire when they made camp.

After many days of travel, the hunters at last caught sight of the huge buffalo herds that filled the land for as far as the eye could see. Before the hunt could start, they held a feast and prayed for success.

The hunters rode into the midst of the thundering herds which was dangerous work and required skill and bravery. Guns were fired at the animals and as the hunters galloped along, they reloaded their weapons to fire again. The buffalo was an important resource. Each buffalo could yield as much as 1,000 pounds of meat. The hunters dried and smoked the meat to preserve it. The hides were staked to the ground and allowed to dry. The Sauk and Meskwaki traded some of the hides to other tribes but kept some for themselves, using them in the winter as blankets and as door coverings for their winter houses.

FOREST

The Sauk and Meskwaki had lived in forested areas for as long as they could remember and knew how best to utilize their resources. The mature trees were huge; many were hundreds of years old. The Sauk and Meskwaki called the trees Grandfathers and honored their Spirits. The trees provided wood for houses, canoes, and fire. When a tree was cut down, the people left an offering of tobacco to the tree's Spirit. It was a way to honor the Grandfather and to thank the Spirit for providing materials so that the people could survive. Men did all the hunting. Boys began hunting in the forests when they were ten years old. Their fathers and uncles taught them to be good hunters. They taught the boys how to track the animals, how to read their tracks and other signs they left, how to move noiselessly through the forest, and how to wait patiently for their chance to make a shot. When they had killed an animal, the boys were taught to give thanks to the animal's Spirit for sacrificing itself so that the people could live. Though guns were used to hunt in the forest, the bow and arrow still was in use, too. An arrow, unlike a gun, made little noise.

Deer were a main forest resource providing meat, skins from which to make leather, and bones and antlers for making tools. Wild turkeys, squirrels, and bears also were hunted for food. Bear meat was a favorite food. The bear's fat was melted down and used as a hair dressing and smeared on the skin as an insect repellant. Oiled bear skins were used as waterproof coverings.

Women tanned the deer and other animal

hides. The hide was removed and stretched out on a frame. The inside of the hide was cleaned with bone scrapers. Wood ashes and water were mixed to make lye which was applied to the hairy side of the hide. The lye loosened the hair making it easy to remove. The hide was scraped to remove any leftover bits of hair. Then the hide was washed and stretched out to dry. Cooked deer brains were rubbed into the stiff, dried hides to soften them. Finally, the women smoked the hides over a fire for several days. The tanned hides were used to make clothing, storage bags and other items. Girls learned these skills by watching, listening, and helping in the process.

The women and girls collected many plants from the forests that were used for food, medicines, and dyes. The girls listened carefully to learn which plants were safe to use and which were poisonous. The girls were taught that when it was necessary to dig a plant out of the ground, they should leave an offering of tobacco to the Spirit of the Earth. The girls learned the proper songs to sing as they made the plants into medicines.

Wild Ginger root was used to flavor foods. The root could be mashed and used to treat infected wounds.

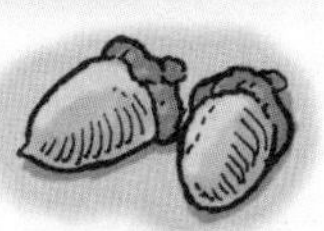

White oak acorns were roasted, pounded into flour, and made into bread. The bark could be used for tanning animal hides. Walnuts, wild grapes, and strawberries also were gathered.

Mayapple fruits were collected and eaten. The rest of the mayapple plant could not be eaten because it was poisonous, but the root could be mashed up and used to treat warts.

Bloodroot could not be eaten because it was poisonous, but the root could be mashed up and put on painful wounds. The red juice in the root was used to make dye.

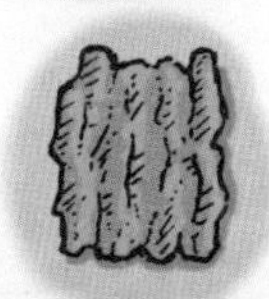

Hickory trees provided nuts. The bark was used to smoke meat and animal hides. The wood was used to make bows, lacrosse stick handles, and drumsticks.

The wood of the basswood tree was used to make bowls, spoons, and other wooden objects. The inner bark was stripped off, soaked in water and then pounded. It was twisted into twine which was used to make storage and collection bags, fish nets, and rope.

RIVER BOTTOM

River bottom

Sturgeon

Fishing with woven net

Midsummer Moon was the time for hunting, fishing and collecting cattails and reeds. The men and boys did the hunting and fishing. The rivers teemed with river sturgeon, bass, and trout. Living near the river rapids made fishing easier. Men cast basswood fiber nets to catch fish or speared the fish in the shallow water. The fish were dried on platforms. The men and boys hunted crayfish and turtles. They shot ducks, geese, and swans. The meat was eaten, and the feathers were used to line clothing for softness and warmth.

Dugout canoes were made from basswood, black walnut, or pine. The men cut down the trees, removed the branches, and dragged the logs back to the town where the canoes were made. The bark was stripped off, and the bottom of the log was made flat. Hot coals were placed down the center of the top, allowing the wood to burn slowly. The fire was put out, and a metal tool called an adze was used to dig out the charred wood. The process was repeated until the canoe was finished. Dugout canoes could be up to fifty feet long, capable of carrying a dozen people and their belongings. People knelt in the canoes. The men propelled them by the use of poles and paddles.

While the men were hunting and fishing, the women were busy collecting other food resources. They waded into the river and used basswood fiber nets to scoop up river mussels. The mussel shells were opened to remove the meat. Some of the shells were made into

Burning out a dugout canoe

Mussel

tools. Some women harvested the fleshy roots of the bear potato and swan root plants which grew in the damp, rich soils along the rivers. Some of the roots were eaten right away, but most were sliced and dried and saved to be eaten during the winter. Some women collected cattails, reeds, and bulrushes that grew in the marshes. The children helped spread out the plants to dry. The leaves were woven into mats for floors and beds. Sometimes the leaves were dyed to make the mats more attractive. The dried stalks and leaves of the cattails were sewn together tightly with basswood twine to make mats that were used to cover their winter houses. Every summer a woman wove over 300 mats for her family's use during the upcoming year.

Gathering eggs

Gathering reeds

Weaving rush mats

ewing reeds ogether to nake mats

one needle

Basket making with basswood fibers

LEAD COUNTRY

Lead musket balls

Mississippi River bluffs

Some Sauk and Meskwaki families moved north to work the lead mines. It took nearly a week to make the 100 mile journey by canoe from Saukenuk. They looked forward to seeing their relatives who lived at the mines. As they traveled, they saw hawks, turkey vultures, ospreys and eagles soaring above the river. Eagles were sacred to them, and it seemed a good sign that they were watching over the people. As they neared the lead country, ancient rocks towered above them on both sides of the river. They called the rocks Grandfathers because they were the oldest things on earth. Their Spirits watched over the people, too.

The area to which the people were going was rich in lead ore deposits. The Meskwaki had summer towns located near the mines. For many years the Sauk and Meskwaki had relied on the lead to trade for goods. Lead was a valuable metal to the Americans. Lead was used to manufacture many items including bullets, paint, pewter, and glass.

By 1817 the Sauk and Meskwaki produced over 400,000 pounds of lead each year, worth $8,000 in trade goods. Losing the mines would be a serious loss. The Meskwaki were especially protective of their lead mines located on

Dubuque mines

the west bank of the Mississippi River. They nearly had been cheated out of these mines by men who lived in St. Louis. No white people were welcome near their town or mines now.

Both men and women participated in the mining process. The men dug the ore, and the women smelted it to extract the lead. Ore near the surface was chipped out with bone or iron hoes.

Mokuk basket

Breaking up lead ore and smelting out the metal in a fire

Ore embedded in rock was more difficult to remove. The miners heated the rock and then poured cold water on it, causing the rock to crack. The crack was opened with crowbars, and the ore was removed in chunks. The ore was loaded into baskets made of bark or rawhide and hauled to the smelting fires. The women built huge fires into which they threw the chunks of ore. The heat from the fire caused the lead in the ore to melt. The melted lead ran down into small depressions dug in the ground. As the lead cooled, it hardened into small pieces called plats.

Lead plat

LATE SUMMER

As Midsummer Moon ended and Elk Moon began to grow, the Sauk and Meskwaki who had left two months earlier returned to their summer towns. As the buffalo hunters wound their way back from the prairies and entered the town, they were welcomed joyfully. They brought large amounts of dried meat and many buffalo robes. Now there was plenty of meat for everyone and enough robes to last the whole winter. The buffalo robes kept the people warm during the winter nights. They were spread out to sleep on and hung over the doorways of the winter houses to keep out snow and cold air.

Other groups returned by canoe. Those who had been in the marshes brought back cattails, reeds, and the delicious swan root and bear potato roots. Those who had been fishing brought back dried river sturgeon, trout, and catfish. As they returned, people shouted with joy at seeing relatives who had been gone for so long.

When everyone had returned, they gathered and exchanged gifts. Ritual gift giving was a long established tradition among the Sauk and Meskwaki. It was a way of sharing,

Return from the buffalo hunt

Scene at the canoe landing

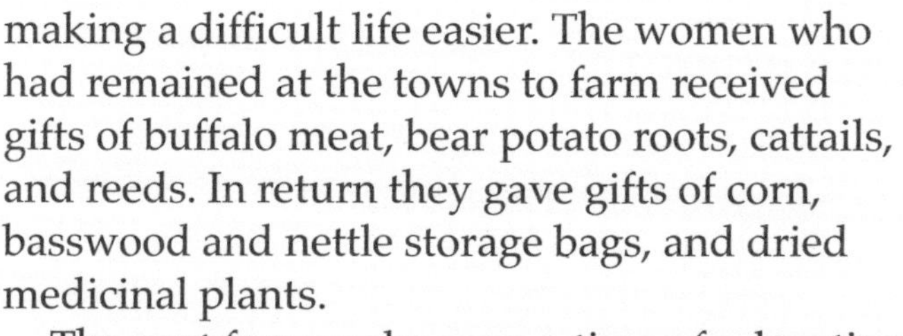

Feast bowl

making a difficult life easier. The women who had remained at the towns to farm received gifts of buffalo meat, bear potato roots, cattails, and reeds. In return they gave gifts of corn, basswood and nettle storage bags, and dried medicinal plants.

The next few weeks were a time of relaxation while they waited for the corn to ripen. The women played bone dice. The men raced their horses and canoes.

Feasting and gift giving

Lacrosse players

During this time they played lacrosse, their great summer ball game. Men and women played separately. Each moiety formed a team, sometimes numbering over 100 players each. Each player carried a lacrosse stick. The game began when the leather ball was thrown into the air and one team gained possession. The lacrosse stick was used to move the ball downfield. Of course, the opposing team tried to steal the ball. A point was scored when the ball was driven across the goal line. It took four points to win the game.

Finally the sweet corn was ready to eat! The clans took turns hosting harvest feasts. Harvest dances were held in the plaza. It was important to honor Grandmother Earth for her blessings. Now the hard work of harvesting could begin.

Lacrosse stick & ball

HARVEST

The crops finished ripening during Elk Moon. Once the harvest feasts were done, the women set to work. All the vegetables had to be harvested and dried during the next few weeks. At Saukenuk and at Wapala's town over 2000 women and children worked together to accomplish these tasks.

The vegetables were collected into baskets and bags and taken to the drying places located near the houses in the farm fields. Drying was their only method of food preservation. As long as the vegetables were kept dry, they would not spoil and would last all year. The corn was either lightly roasted or pounded into meal. The beans were hung up in large bunches on drying racks, and the pumpkins and squashes were hollowed out, cut into rings, and suspended from poles to dry. Later the dried vegetables could be cooked by adding water and making them into soup.

As the harvest was ending, the people began to prepare for winter. In just a few weeks everyone would leave the summer towns and go to their winter hunting grounds. They would be gone all winter. Most of the dried food was taken along to eat. Some of the food, along with the seeds needed to plant next Planting Moon, was left at the towns, hidden in underground storage pits called caches.

The caches were located near the long houses, often inside under the benches. To prepare the cache, the women dug a hole two feet wide and three feet deep. Cold ashes were spread around the interior and covered with layers of bark. The dried food and seeds were put into fiber bags made of basswood, nettle, or cedar. Cedar bags were preferred as they naturally repelled insects. The bags were placed inside and then covered with another layer of bark. The remainder of the hole was filled with clay. A fire was lit on top of the clay to harden it and to keep moisture out. Now the dried food and seeds would remain safe from insects and wild animals while the people were away for the winter. The women took care to hide the traces of the locations of the cache pits. Sometimes humans came into the empty summer towns, and if they found the hidden food, they stole it.

THE FUR TRADERS

While the women were busy harvesting, the men planned for the winter hunt. They needed guns and ammunition, new axes and knives, and new woolen blankets which they got from their traders. The traders gave out the goods on credit in the fall with the promise of payment with animal pelts in the spring. For over 150 years the Sauk and Meskwaki had traded with the French from St. Louis and the English from Canada. By 1817 the two tribes relied heavily on the trade goods for survival. The chiefs recently had heard that the Americans no longer would allow the English to trade with them. The old traders were their friends, men they trusted. Uncertainty was in the air, and the hunters waited anxiously to see what would happen.

The hunters were surprised when they saw two boats filled with strangers approach the canoe landing. As the boats drew closer, the hunters relaxed. They recognized two of the traders as old friends, but the others in the boat were new to them. They had been sent by the newly formed American Fur Company. They had brought their goods all the way from Mackinac Island, traveling for more than four weeks to reach Saukenuk. They had traveled across Lake Michigan, through Wisconsin, and down the Mississippi River.

The man in charge of the expedition, Russel Farnham, was new to the Mississippi River valley. He was eager to make a success of his first venture here.

Fur trade canoe

Farnham opened up the boxes and spread his wares out for the hunters to inspect: rifles and shotguns; gunpowder and powder horns; gunflints and lead to make bullets; steel axes and knives; and iron muskrat and fish spears. For the women he had bolts of brightly colored woolen and cotton cloth, needles and thimbles, scissors, and sewing silk. Farnham set out bright copper and brass kettles, woolen blankets and shawls, colored silk ribbon, silk handkerchiefs, silver arm bands and earrings, mirrors, glass beads, and playing cards. Clothing made from scarlet woolen cloth and vermillion that was used to make highly prized, red paint, were available too.

Once the trader's clerk carefully had recorded their purchases on credit, the hunters could leave for the winter hunt. Farnham packed up his remaining goods and also prepared to follow them into their winter hunting grounds.

Obtaining goods on credit

DEPARTING IN FALL

First Frosty Moon was here. The harvest was nearly finished, and the traders had come and gone. The Sauk and Meskwaki prepared to leave their summer towns for the winter hunt as they did every year. Winter required so much fuel and meat to keep the population of the large summer towns warm and fed that it made sense to break apart in smaller bands, ranging in size from thirty to seventy families, to survive more easily. Once the fur trade was established, the two tribes had another reason to depart—to gather as many furs as possible to be able to purchase as many goods as possible.

The people began to pack up whatever they would need to survive the next seven months. The dried food was packed up in deerskin bags. The cattail mats and red elm bark used to cover their winter homes were rolled carefully and tied with lengths of basswood and nettle rope. Cooking gear, guns, knives, blankets, and medicines were packed, too.

Packing up to depart

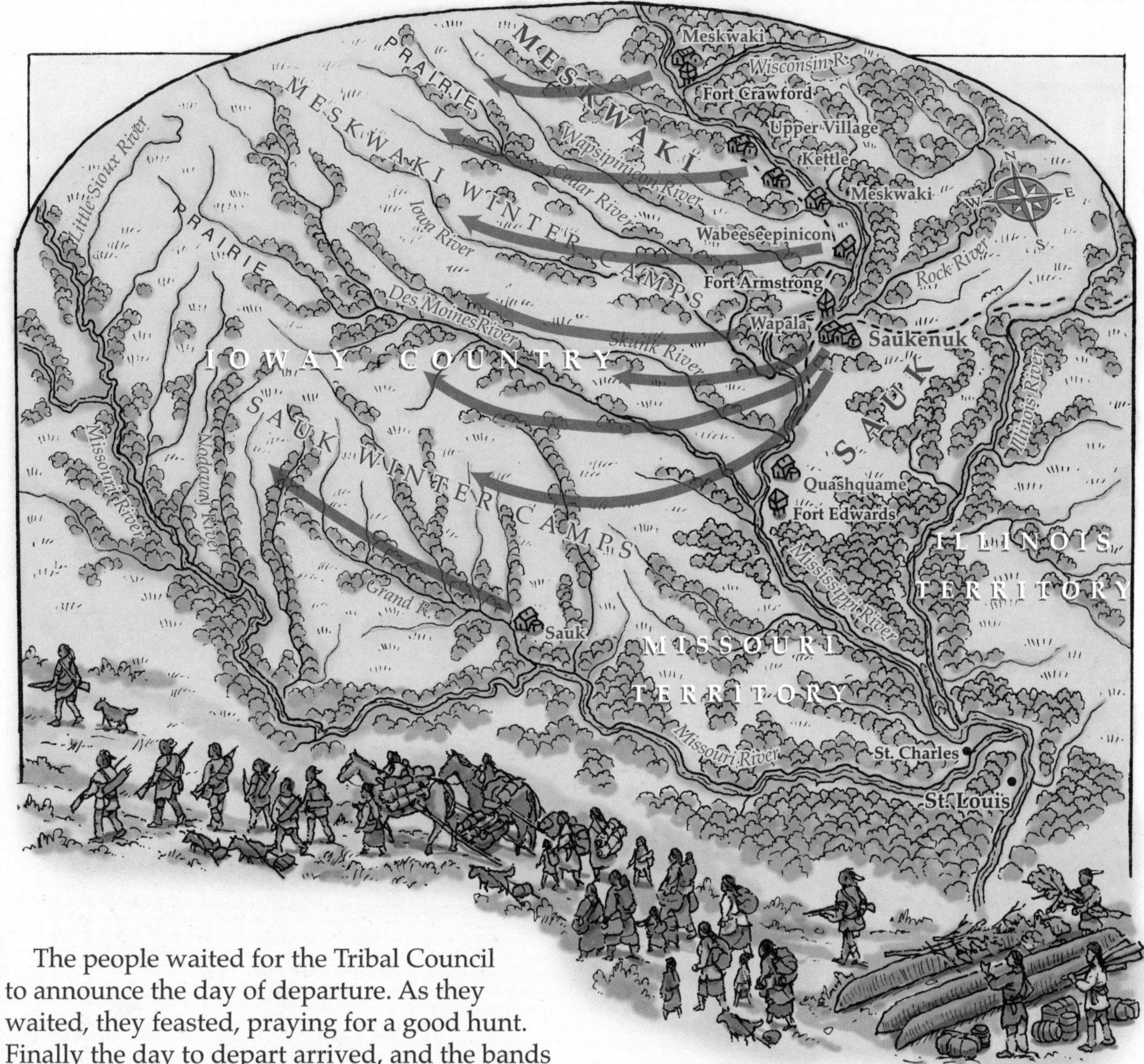

The people waited for the Tribal Council to announce the day of departure. As they waited, they feasted, praying for a good hunt. Finally the day to depart arrived, and the bands began to move out. Each band was assigned a hunting area by the Tribal Council. The vast hunting territory belonged to the entire nation, not just an individual band. Many bands traveled by canoe down the Mississippi River to the mouths of the Iowa, Skunk, and Des Moines Rivers, then went upstream to reach their hunting grounds. Some continued further south into the Missouri Territory to the Salt River valley. Those who had horses traveled as far west as the Missouri River.

Their traders followed the bands into the interior, establishing temporary posts for themselves. Often the hunting bands left their more elderly members with the traders who cared for and protected them. The bands left their canoes at the trader's post, hoisted their belongings onto their backs, and moved into the interior. Within a few weeks they would reach their winter camp locations so that they could be settled before the weather turned cold.

THE WINTER CAMP

RUTTING MOON - FREEZING MOON
1817
October 10 — December 7

Winter camps were located in the river valleys. The trees provided fuel, building materials, and protection from the weather. The rivers provided water for drinking and cooking. The hunting bands lived in the winter camps for the next four months until the end of Little Bear Moon.

Each winter house, called a wickiup, was small and round and used by one family. The wickiup measured about twenty feet in diameter and about twelve feet tall. It was made of a frame of woven saplings, bent over with their ends driven into the ground. The Meskwaki preferred to cover the frame with red elm bark, while the Sauk preferred using cattail mats. A fire pit was dug in the center of the house, and the bed of hot coals kept the wickiups warm even on the coldest day. Reed mats and buffalo robes were laid on the ground to provide comfort for sleeping. A large buffalo robe covered the doorway.

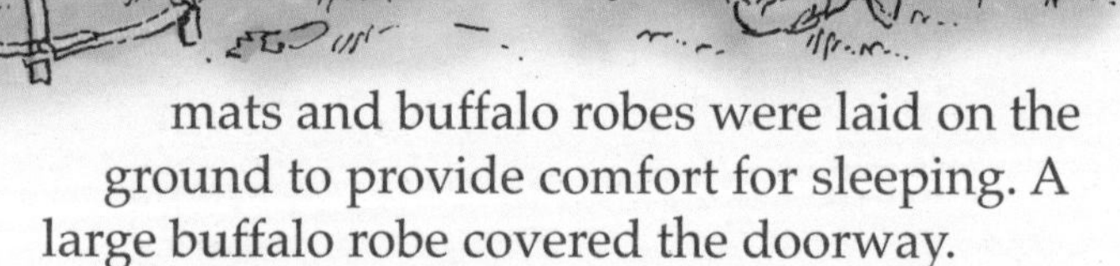

Constructing wickiups

The women unpacked the kettles, knives, axes, and bags of dried food they had brought from the summer towns. The bags of food were hung from the rafters to keep out the mice. The firewood that had been gathered was stacked near the house and covered with an oiled bearskin to keep it dry. The men went out to hunt and the animals they caught provided meat to add to the dried foods. The hunters wore snowshoes when necessary so that they

Hunter on snowshoes

could move quickly over deep snow.

Winter was story telling time. The Sauk and Meskwaki had no written language so knowledge was shared by telling stories. Stories taught the children about their history, religious beliefs, and traditions. Some stories were about the animals and other creatures who shared the rivers, forests, and prairies with them. The stories were entertaining and helped pass the long winter nights. The children listened attentively as the winter winds howled outside. Repetition helped the children to learn the stories by heart. Those adults who had excellent memories were responsible for remembering and repeating the stories. This oral tradition preserved the information so that it could be shared from one generation to the next.

Inside a wickiup on a cold winter night

GATHERING FURS

BIG BEAR MOON - LITTLE BEAR MOON
1817-1818
December 8 — February 4

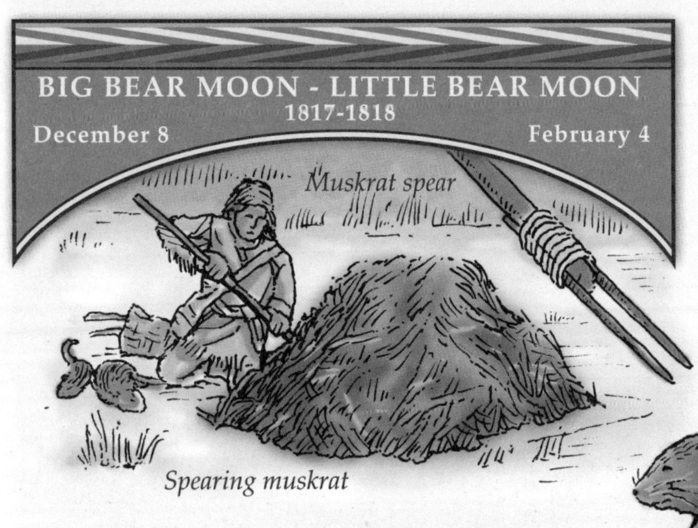

Spearing muskrat

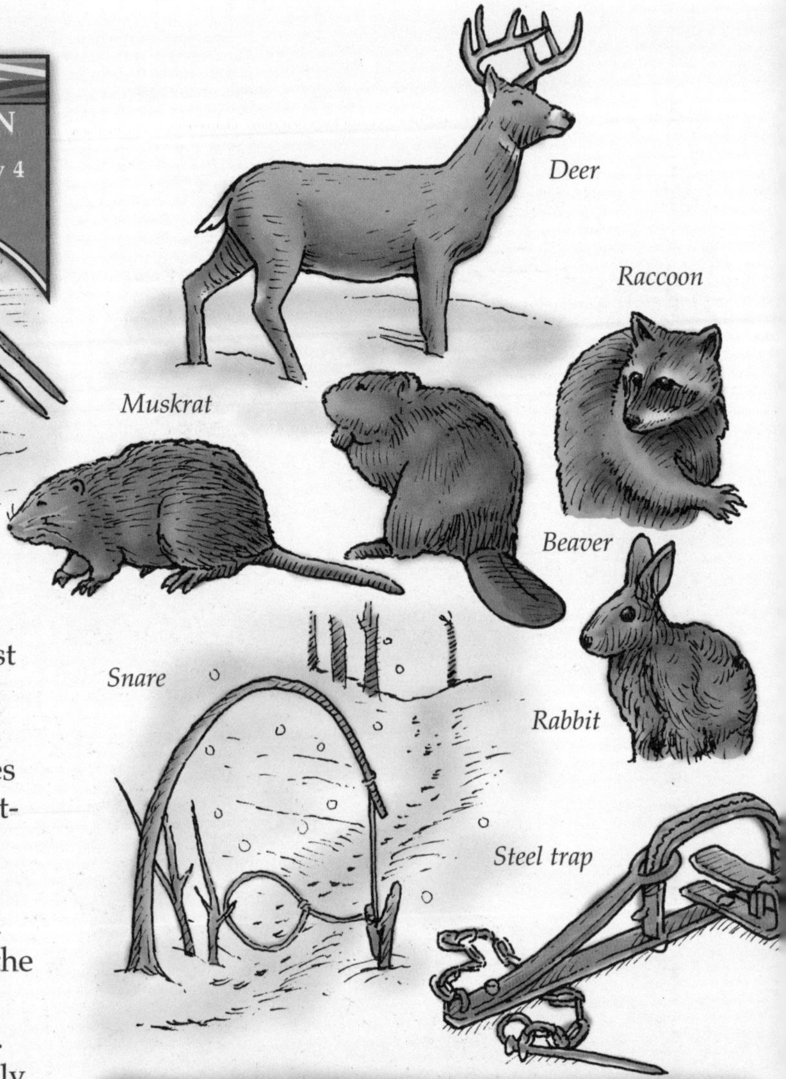

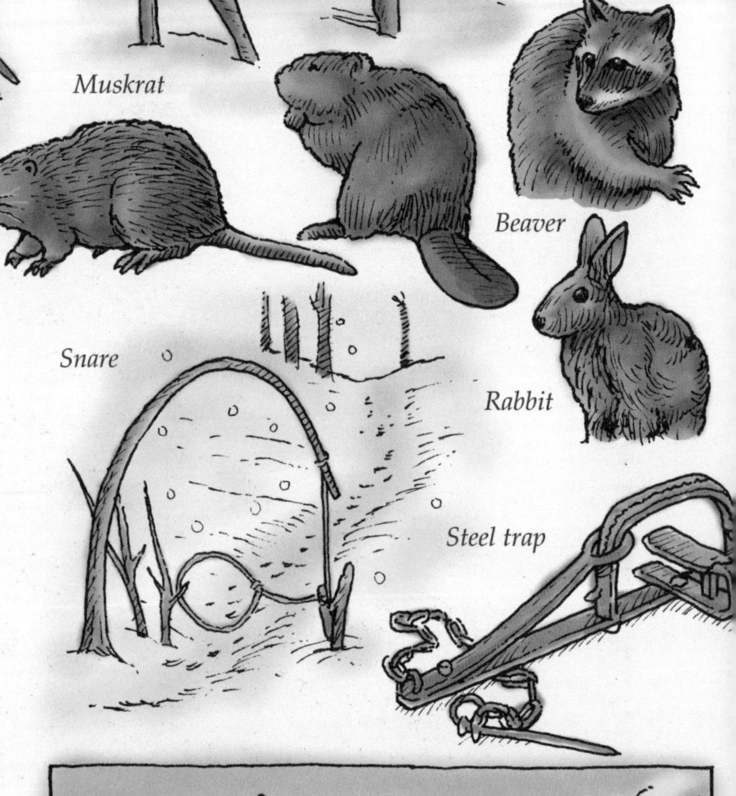

Hunting began during Rutting Moon and continued through the end of Big Bear Moon. The animals' furs were at their thickest at this time. The hunting grounds were filled with deer, muskrat, mink, raccoon, and otter. The prairie edges, forests, rivers, and marshes provided a perfect habitat for them. The hunters used guns, iron muskrat spears, and iron traps which rapidly were replacing the old trapping and hunting methods of snares and deadfalls. The hunters hauled their catch to the winter camps where the women skinned the animals and cleaned and stretched the hides. The dried skins or pelts were stacked carefully, ready to be given to their traders to pay off their fall credits.

Big Bear Moon was the best time to hunt muskrats that lived in winter dens built in ponds and marshes. When the water froze, the hunters could walk across the ice and insert their muskrat spears into the den.

Mr. Farnham and his crew established their winter camp along the Des Moines River, building and living in a log cabin. Farnham visited the different bands periodically to collect the pelts and to restock supplies of ammunition. He carried the pelts back to his winter house where they were counted and credited to each hunter's account. Farnham was pleased with the number of pelts he had collected so far. Once he had collected the furs from the spring beaver and bear hunt, he would load them into canoes and take them back to Mackinac Island. In time, the pelts would be sold in the fur markets around the world.

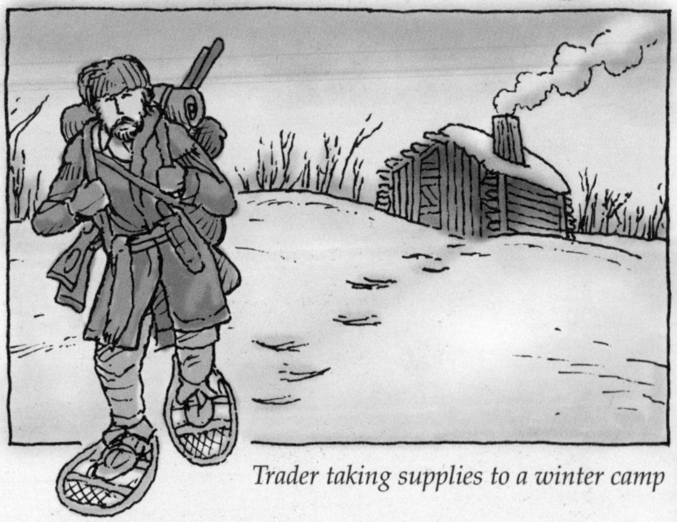

Trader taking supplies to a winter camp

Black bear emerging from hibernation

During the month of Little Bear Moon, the weather worsened and the animals' furs were not as thick. The hunters returned to the winter camp where they remained all month, passing the time by playing cards. As the month drew to an end, some of the people prepared to depart the camp. The men would continue hunting beaver and bear. The women, children, and elderly prepared to move to the sugar maple groves. They packed up their belongings and took down the red elm bark and cattail mats that covered the wickiups, carefully packing them to be used when they got to the sugar camp. They said goodbye to their husbands, fathers, and sons. Two months would pass before they would see them again, but Cold Moon was here. It was time to go.

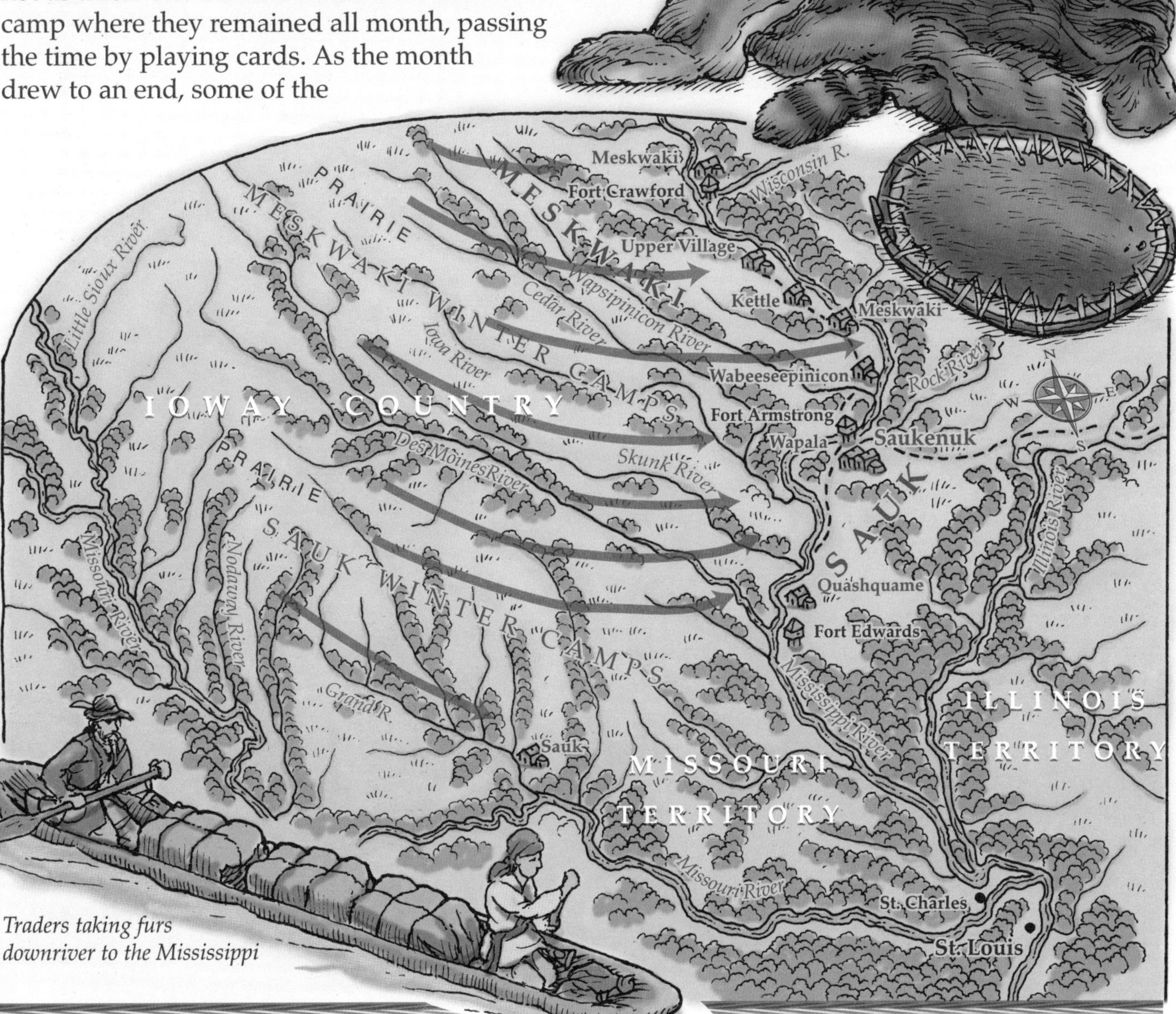

Pelts

Traders taking furs downriver to the Mississippi

THE SUGAR CAMP

Sap Moon—the time when it was cold in the morning and warm in the afternoon—was the time to collect the maple tree's sap. The people would remain at the sugar camps for the next several weeks. It was a happy time of year. Life was beginning inside the trees, and soon winter would be over.

The women owned the sugar groves, returning to the same ones each year. When the people arrived at the grove, the women built new wickiups using the old cattail mats and bark to cover them. Children collected firewood and fresh sumac branches from the forest. The sumac branches were hollowed out and made into spiles that were used to drain the sap from the tree. Others brought out the sugaring materials stored at the grove—large copper kettles, bark mokuks, and stirring paddles.

Once all was ready, the people held a feast and prayed for a good sugaring season. Four days later the work began. Everyone helped. Sugaring season could be brief. The trees were tapped, and the sap was collected and brought back to the fires where it was boiled down into syrup and then sugar. The sugar was packed carefully into mokuks, ready to be taken back to the summer towns to be used throughout the

year. Sugar was used to flavor meats, vegetables, and stews. On hot summer days it was dissolved in water to make a sweet, refreshing drink.

Sometimes a big snowfall came. The children knew they were in for a treat. Some of the thick syrup was poured into the snow to cool it off quickly, turning it into candy. They only got candy once a year and were so happy.

When the sap stopped flowing, sugaring time was done. The people had another feast to celebrate a good sugaring season. After the feast everyone could eat as much sugar as they wanted. It was a time of joy. As the days grew longer, they patiently waited for the signs that would tell them it was time to leave.

Now the signs were there. The sap had stopped flowing out from the maple trees, the buds on the trees were starting to open, the ice was breaking up in the rivers, and the first frogs could be heard croaking. It was time for the people to return to their summer towns and begin the cycle of the seasons again.

Leaving the sugar camp for the gathering

CRISIS AND LOSS

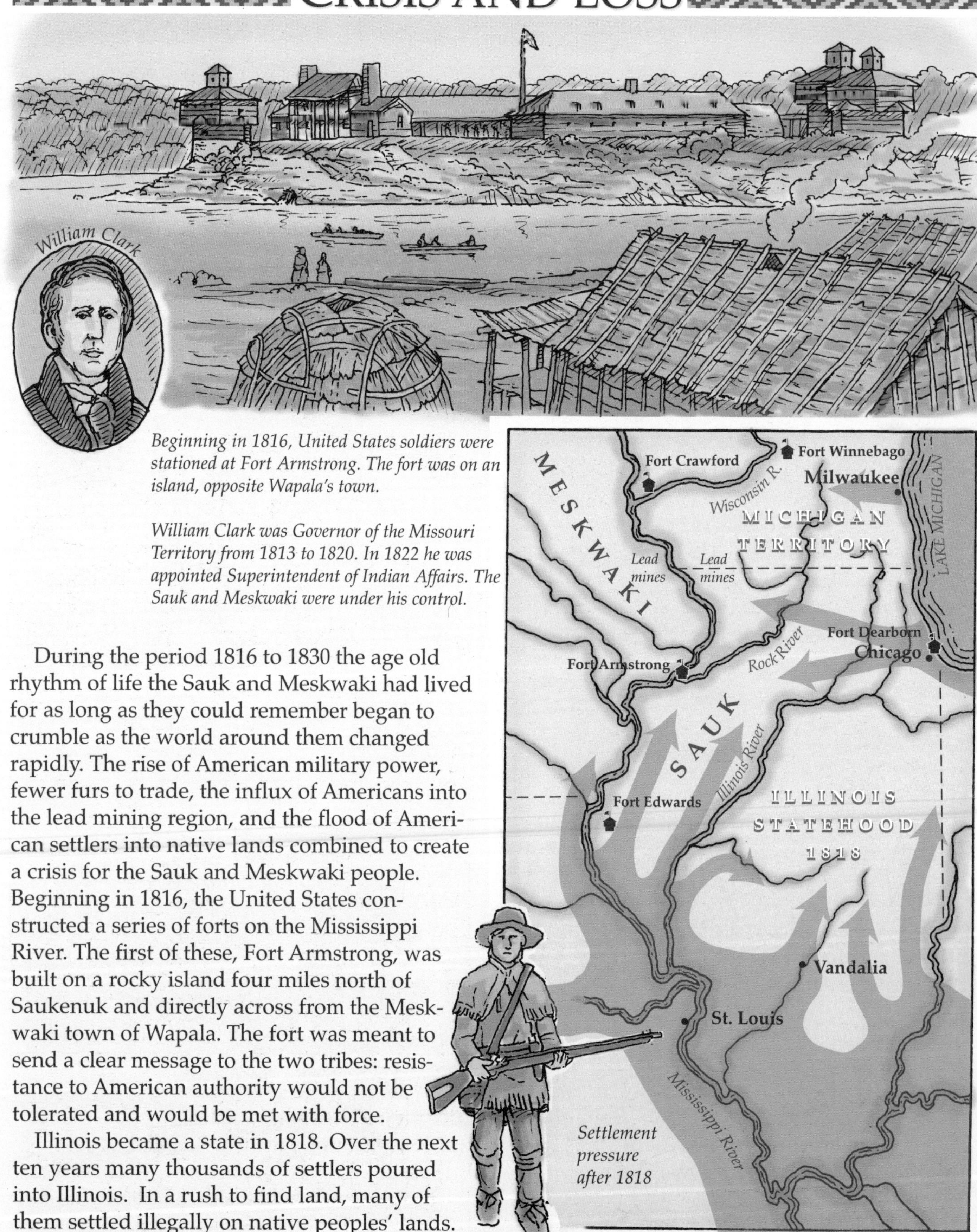

Beginning in 1816, United States soldiers were stationed at Fort Armstrong. The fort was on an island, opposite Wapala's town.

William Clark was Governor of the Missouri Territory from 1813 to 1820. In 1822 he was appointed Superintendent of Indian Affairs. The Sauk and Meskwaki were under his control.

During the period 1816 to 1830 the age old rhythm of life the Sauk and Meskwaki had lived for as long as they could remember began to crumble as the world around them changed rapidly. The rise of American military power, fewer furs to trade, the influx of Americans into the lead mining region, and the flood of American settlers into native lands combined to create a crisis for the Sauk and Meskwaki people. Beginning in 1816, the United States constructed a series of forts on the Mississippi River. The first of these, Fort Armstrong, was built on a rocky island four miles north of Saukenuk and directly across from the Meskwaki town of Wapala. The fort was meant to send a clear message to the two tribes: resistance to American authority would not be tolerated and would be met with force.

Illinois became a state in 1818. Over the next ten years many thousands of settlers poured into Illinois. In a rush to find land, many of them settled illegally on native peoples' lands.

Rather than remove the illegal settlers, the United States government insisted the various tribes give up their lands and move west of the Mississippi River. This policy was given official status with the passage of the Indian Removal Act of 1830.

During the 1820's the fur trade, so critical to the Sauk and Meskwaki economy, began to collapse. Years of overhunting, the pressures of Americans settling on tribal hunting grounds, and increased competition with other native nations caused game to become increasingly scarce. Territorial disputes between the Sauk and Meskwaki and the Dakota led to war. When hunting camps were attacked, the Sauk and Meskwaki were forced to abandon them. The women, children, and elderly were moved to places of safety while the warriors moved out to fight. No one could hunt in safety. Successive poor winter hunts left the two tribes unable to pay off their credits to their traders.

By 1830 the Sauk and Meskwaki were over $50,000 in debt to their traders.

In 1822 four Americans were granted a lease by the American government to mine the lead found east of the Mississippi River. The Sauk and Meskwaki were told they no longer could mine in Illinois, causing a devastating loss to their economy. The prospect of riches brought on a "lead rush," and by 1828 over 8,000 Americans had flocked to Illinois seeking to make their fortunes. Some of them illegally expanded their mining onto lands still owned by various native nations, causing tensions between the native people and the Americans. In 1829 the American government took the disputed lands in a series of forced treaties. American officials now wanted the Meskwaki lead mines at Dubuque on the west bank of the Mississippi River and repeatedly pressured the Meskwaki to sell them. The Meskwaki refused to sell.

In March 1829 while the Sauk and Meskwaki were away on the winter hunt, several white families moved into Saukenuk. The Sauk were astounded upon their return to find strangers living in their long houses and plowing up their cornfields. The white people had no legal right to live there. Yet, American officials told the chiefs of the two tribes that they must abandon their towns on the east bank of the Mississippi and move across the river. Most of them reluctantly agreed to go, but a significant faction of Sauk refused to leave the land of their ancestors. Their leader was an elderly Sauk warrior named Black Hawk.

THE BLACK HAWK WAR

Black Hawk was Sauk. He was not a chief. He was a warrior and was recognized within the Sauk nation as the leader of the political faction strongly opposed to removal from Saukenuk. By returning to Saukenuk in the spring of 1830, the faction acted against the wishes of the national chiefs.

Keokuck was Sauk. Though not a chief, he was a brilliant orator and friend to the United States. Throughout the decade of the 1820's, he worked to become friendly with the Americans and to solidify his power among the Sauk. He and Black Hawk became bitter rivals in the political crisis that ended in the Black Hawk War.

The refusal of Black Hawk's band to leave Saukenuk led the United States to take military action resulting in the Black Hawk War of 1832. It was the last Indian war fought east of the Mississippi River.

The American demand in 1829 that the Sauk and Meskwaki abandon their towns on the east bank of the Mississippi River threw the Sauk nation into a political crisis. The national chiefs, with Keokuck serving as their representative, were willing to accept removal in order to avoid war with the Americans. Yet, a significant portion of the tribe, led by Black Hawk, was strongly against removal. The Tribal Council could not reach a consensus, opening a political rift within the nation.

In the spring of 1830, Keokuck's followers made a new town on the Iowa River. Black Hawk's followers returned to Saukenuk, vowing to remain there or die. Black Hawk believed that war with the United States could be avoided if he and his band remained peaceful. Yet, many of the Americans at Saukenuk did not want any Sauk living near them and demanded that they be removed. In the spring of 1831, United States troops and Illinois state militiamen were sent to Saukenuk to remove Black Hawk's band peacefully if possible, by force if necessary. Black Hawk's band was outnumbered and fled across the Mississippi. They returned to Illinois in April 1832, intending to go to the Winnebago Prophet's town on the Rock River to spend the summer there and raise their corn. Black Hawk's band numbered 1,500 people, over 1,000 of them women, children, and elderly. Black Hawk did not intend to wage war. Nevertheless, the United States government regarded the Sauk return as an invasion. The army and state militia were called out and sent to pursue Black Hawk.

The conflict known as the Black Hawk War was brief, lasting less than three months. The war began in error in May at the Battle of Stillman's Run, when state militiamen shot and killed two Sauk men bearing white flags. Black Hawk had sent them to seek a peaceful means

Map of the Black Hawk War, 1832

out of the crisis his return had caused. After the two Sauk were killed, Black Hawk fled with his band into the marshes of the headwaters of the Rock River, hiding out there for the next two months. By July Black Hawk was forced to withdraw because his people had no food and many were sick. They began a desperate retreat across present day Wisconsin, hoping to escape across the Mississippi River. His band reached the River on the evening of August 1, 1832, only to find American forces already there. Again he tried to surrender, and again he was fired upon. The Battle of Bad Axe was fought the next day, and many Sauk were killed.

The war was a disaster for both the Sauk and Meskwaki nations. Over 1,000 Sauk died. The treaty that ended the war punished both tribes. The Meskwaki had neither supported nor been members of Black Hawk's band, but they were punished equally. The United States took a fifty mile wide strip of land on the west bank of the Mississippi River, including the Meskwaki lead mines at Dubuque. This time was a low point in the history of the Sauk and Meskwaki people, but the story does not end there.

THE TWO TRIBES TODAY

In 1842 the Sauk and Meskwaki were forced to cede the remainder of their Iowa lands to the United States government. The treaty required that the two tribes move to a reservation in present day Kansas. The paths of the two tribes began to separate at this time, and by the mid-1850's they ended their political alliance.

Meskwaki National Emblam

The Meskwaki

Some of the Meskwaki refused to leave Iowa. Many went to Kansas but in time returned, and in 1857 with the support of the State of Iowa they purchased eighty acres of land in Tama County. Today the tribe owns 7,700 acres. Unlike a reservation, this land belongs to the Meskwaki and is called a settlement. Meskwaki children attend school on the settlement where they learn the Meskwaki language along with other subjects, such as English, math, and science. Both the Sauk and Meskwaki have jobs similar to other Americans, such as police officers, teachers, lawyers, and doctors. The Meskwaki continue to live by their tribal customs and belief system. They have been able to preserve their identity as a people for their own well being and for the future of their children.

Sauki National Emblam

The Sauk

The Sauk had divided into two factions: the Sauki and the Nemaha. The Nemaha lived along the Missouri River and in 1837 moved to a reservation in Kansas. The Nemaha still live in Kansas and are called the Sac and Fox Nation of Missouri in Kansas and Nebraska.

By 1845 the Sauki had moved to a reservation in Kansas. In 1869 the United States government moved the Sauki to a reservation in present day Oklahoma. Sauk children attend public schools and study the subjects all children do. Both the Sauk and Meskwaki serve in the United States military. Today the Sauki are called the Sac and Fox Nation of Oklahoma. They continue to practice many of their traditional customs, such as clan feasts and adoption ceremonies. Despite the upheavals of the past, the Sauk have retained their identity as a people.

Not all Sauk and Meskwaki live in Oklahoma, Kansas, and Iowa and can be found living across our country. Today the descendants of the Sauk and Meskwaki who once lived and flourished along the Mississippi River valley remain connected as they have been over the centuries, linked through language, customs, traditions, and marriage.